The Editors

Gillian Allnutt is the poetry editor of *City Limits* magazine. Born in London in 1949, she is the author of two books of poetry, *Spitting the Pips Out* and *Beginning the Avocado*.

Fred D'Aguiar was born in London of Guyanese parents in 1958. He has been editorially involved in *Artrage* magazine and has published *Mama Dot*, *Explainer*, an epic poem in defence of the traditions of Black poetry and *Airy Hall*. He has also written two plays, *A Jamaican Airman Foresees His Death* and *High Life*.

Ken Edwards, born in Gibraltar in 1950, is a London-based writer and editor of the influential poetry magazine, *Reality Studios*. His own books include *Drumming & Poems*, *Intensive Care* and *A4 Landscape*.

Eric Mottram is a distinguished poet, critic and teacher. His books include *Elegies*, *A Book of Herne*, *Interrogation Rooms* and the groundbreaking critical study, *William Burroughs: The Algebra of Need*. He is Professor of American Literature at King's College, University of London.

The New British Poetry
1968–88

Edited by
GILLIAN ALLNUTT
FRED D'AGUIAR
KEN EDWARDS
ERIC MOTTRAM

PALADIN
GRAFTON BOOKS
A Division of the Collins Publishing Group

LONDON GLASGOW
TORONTO SYDNEY AUCKLAND

Paladin
Grafton Books
A Division of the Collins Publishing Group
8 Grafton Street, London W1X 3LA

A Paladin Paperback Original 1988

ISBN 0-586-08765-6

Printed and bound in Great Britain by
Collins, Glasgow

Set in Baskerville

'. . . but it is good to be several floors up in the dead of night
   wondering if you are any good or not
and the only decision you can make is that you did it . . .'

Frank O'Hara

■ PUBLISHER'S NOTE

The New British Poetry is a different kind of anthology from others that have appeared from British publishers in recent years, in that it surveys a number of areas in contemporary poetry without attempting to arbitrate between them. The majority of recent anthologies have tended to assert the claims of one particular group, a particular idea about poetry, a shared set of concerns or social experience. Through a combination of circumstance and intention, this approach has led to the more adventurous and hard-hitting kinds of contemporary poetry being marginalized, whilst a narrowly-defined orthodoxy gets on with running the show. The implication is made that these are the 'true' poets, the 'real' poets – even the *only* poets.

This anthology wasn't made that way. Four poet-editors were offered a limited amount of space in which to survey and introduce an important strand in contemporary British poetry to a relatively uncommitted but open-minded reader. They were not asked to be impartial. Their differences, both in the shape they have given their selections and in their introductory remarks, make this a many-sided, exciting, unpredictable – and no doubt contentious book. In placing different traditions side by side, surprising juxtapositions occur and previously unguessed affinities are revealed.

Gillian Allnutt, Fred D'Aguiar, Ken Edwards and Eric Mottram have made use of the twenty year historical frame (1968–88) in a variety of ways: to deny the linearity of literary tradition, to 'mirror' a contemporary scene, to show the subsequent development of poets who began to publish in the exciting, primitively produced small magazines of the 1960s, and to revaluate past work in the light of its inheritors. And that is possibly the most significant aspect of this anthology: the vitality and strength it reveals amongst younger poets across the entire spectrum of British poetry now.

John Muckle
Paladin Poetry

■ ACKNOWLEDGEMENTS

For permission to reprint copyright material the publishers gratefully acknowledge the following:

John Agard for 'Listen Mr Oxford Don' from *Mangoes and Bullets* (Pluto Press, 1985) and 'Half-caste'.
Gillian Allnutt and Virago Press for 'Comfortable Words' and 'Alien' from *Beginning the Avocado* (Virago, 1987).
Iftikhar Arif and Professor Ralph Russell for 'Ghazal' and 'To a Despondent Evening'.
Tony Baker for '(for Geraldine)', 'Storm Clouds' and 'Poem'.
Tim Behrens and Anthony Edkins for 'Someone Else', 'Wedding in the Port', 'Montecastelli Poem' and 'the trees are rustling outside the open window' by Sophie Behrens.
Asa Benveniste and Anvil Press Poetry for 'Certainly Metaphysics', 'Infield Outfield', 'We are one with nature O!' from *Throw Out the Life Line, Lay Out the Corse* (Anvil Press, 1983) and the author for 'Blue Crêpe' and 'An End To It' from *Pommes Poems* (Arc Publications, 1988).
James Berry for 'Old Man in New Country', 'Spirits of Movement', 'New Speaker' and 'Poem for the Wife of an Imprisoned Leader'.
Valerie Bloom for 'Longsight Market'.
Eavan Boland and Carcanet Press for 'The Oral Tradition' and 'Nocturne' from *The Journey* (Carcanet, 1987).
Jean Binta Breeze for 'Riddym Ravings (The Mad Woman's Poem)' from *Riddym Ravings and other poems* (Race Today Publications, 1988).
Paul Brown for a selection from 'De Rebus' from the booklet of the same name (Pre-Texts, 1986).
Richard Caddel for 'Wyatt's Dream', 'Two Movements Which Begin At The Head And End At The Feet', 'Going Home' from *Sweet Cicely* (Taxus Press, 1983, reprinted Galloping Dog, 1988), 'Translation From A Lost Source', 'Vers Negre', 'Enchanter's Nightshade', 'Uncertain Steps' and 'The Paths'.
B. Catling for *Boschlog* (A Few Goats Press, 1987).
Faustin Charles for 'Omens of the Morning'.

Cris Cheek for a selection from 'drawing on the traditions' originally published in *A Present* (Bluff Books, 1980).

Thomas A. Clark for five poems from *Sixteen Sonnets* and three poems from *Twenty Poems* (Moschatel Press, 1981 and Grosseteste Press, 1983).

Bob Cobbing for 'Worm', 'tan', 'Alphabet of Fishes', and work from 'Three Poems for Voice and Movement', 'Beethoven Today' and 'Blotting Music', originally published by Writers Forum.

Merle Collins for 'Callaloo' from *Because the Dawn Breaks* (Karia Press, 1985).

Kelvin Corcoran for 'Volitionist Economics' and 'A Slogan Will Not Suffice' from *Robin Hood in the Dark Ages* (Permanent Press, 1985) and 'Nobody Thinks Hard Enough for Poetry' and 'Two Poems' from *Qirat Sepher* (Galloping Dog Press, 1988).

Jeni Couzyn and Bloodaxe Books Ltd for 'Dawn', 'Cartography of the Subtle Heart' and 'The Message' from *Life by Drowning* (Bloodaxe, 1985).

Andrew Crozier for poems from 'High Zero', 'Humiliation in its Disguises' and 'Permanent Wave' from *All Where Each Is* (Allardyce, Barnett, 1985) © Andrew Crozier 1978, 1985.

David Dabydeen and Dangaroo Press for 'Coolie Odyssey' and 'Coolie Mother' from *Slave Song* (Dangaroo Press, 1984).

Carol Ann Duffy and Anvil Press Poetry for 'The Dolphins', 'Telephoning Home' and 'Foreign' from *Selling Manhattan* (Anvil Press, 1987).

Andrew Duncan for 'The Poet and the Schizophrenic' and 'In the Red Grove' from *Threads of Iron*.

Ken Edwards for 'You must change your life', 'The Firmament Doth Shake', 'Geraniums, South London' from *Drumming & Poems* (Galloping Dog Press, 1982).

Paul Evans for 'Ode', 'Two Sonnets', 'Infamous Doctrine' from *The Manual for the Perfect Organisation of Journeys* (Oasis Books, 1979), 'Ode to Tennis' from *Sweet Lucy* (Pig Press, 1983) and selections from 'The Sofa Book' (Arc Publications, 1987).

Alison Fell for 'Medusa on Skyros' and 'Freeze-frame' and Virago Press for 'August 6, 1945' from *Kisses for Mayakovsky* (Virago, 1984).

Peter Finch and Poetry Wales Press for 'The Computer's First proverbs', 'Passion Shaved Beneath the Grain-Silo' and 'Customize the Grass' from *Selected Poems* (Poetry Wales Press, 1987).

Allen Fisher for 'The gardener's preface' from *Unpolished Mirrors*

(Reality Studios, 1985) and 'Birdland' from *Brixton Fractals* (Aloes Books, 1985) © Allen Fisher 1979, 1981, 1985.

Roy Fisher and Oxford University Press for 'On the Open Side', 'Emblem' and a selection from 'Wonders of Obligation' from *Collected Poems 1955–1987* (Oxford University Press, 1988).

Errol Francis for 'Rotogravure', 'Tangerine Sky' and 'If Only'.

Ulli Freer for 'Take the Toys from the Boys' from *Micro Brigade* (1984).

Gabriel Gbadamosi for 'Flying Home', 'The Boat Passage', 'Padraic's Point' and 'The Sewing Box'.

Glenda George for 'QUASI, QUASI . . . as if, repeated' © Glenda George 1980.

Angie Gilligan for 'Household Dilemma', 'BATHSHEBA' and 'Mortgage'.

Bill Griffiths for 'To Tom Saunders on his Imprisonment', 'Terzetto: Brixton', 'Animal', and 'Into Prison' from *War With Windsor* (Pirate Press, 1973) and 'After Stroke', 'For P. Celtic' and 'Compass Poem' from *Tract Against the Giants* (Coach House Press, 1984).

Caroline Halliday for 'Music' and 'ode to my daughter's plimsolls and the mess in her room'.

Lee Harwood for 'As Your Eyes Are Blue . . .' from *The White Room* (Fulcrum Press, 1968), 'Animal Days' from *The Sinking Colony* (Fulcrum Press, 1970) and 'Text for a Poster (2)' from *Monster Masks* (Pig Press, 1985).

Ralph Hawkins for 'The Colours He Came To See', 'Cattle' and 'Birds' from *Tell Me No More And Tell Me* (Grosseteste Press, 1981) and 'Imperfect Air' from *At Last Away* (Galloping Dog Press, 1988).

David Haynes for 'Mediatrix'.

A. L. Hendriks and Savacou for 'Recollections of the Sun' from *The Islanders* (Savacou, 1983).

Selima Hill for 'Crossing the Desert in a Pram' and Chatto & Windus Ltd for 'The Ram' from *Saying Hello at the Station* and 'Looking for Camels' from *My Darling Camel* (Chatto, 1984 and 1988).

Roger Garfitt and Bloodaxe Books Ltd for 'In Painswick Churchyard', 'Irthing Valley', 'Rain – Birdoswald' by Frances Horovitz from *Collected Poems* (Bloodaxe Books in association with The Enitharmon Press, 1985).

Libby Houston for 'A House', 'Judging Lear' and 'Scales' from *At the Mercy* (Allison and Busby, 1981).

Jeff Nuttall for 'The Whore of Kilpeck' from *Poems 1962–68* (Fulcrum Press, 1969) and 'Three Scenes: Todmorden', 'Dub Eleven' from *Scenes and Dubs* (Writers Forum, 1987).

Douglas Oliver for 'The Oracle of the Drowned', 'Snowdonia at a Distance', 'The Ferry Pirate' from *Kind* collected poems 1967–87 (Allardyce, Barnett, 1987) and a selection from *The Infant and the Pearl* (Silver Hounds for Ferry Press, 1985).

Albie Ollivierre for 'Voice' and 'Talk War' from *Tribes*.

Maggie O'Sullivan for 'Lottery & Requiem' and 'Busk, Pierce' from *States of Emergency* (ICPA, 1987).

Evangeline Paterson and Taxus Press for 'Tribal Homeland', 'Dispossessed', 'In a South African Museum' from *Bringing the Water Hyacinth to Africa* (Taxus, 1983).

Tom Pickard for 'valentine', 'recipe: pastime for the unemployed', 'dawn raid in an orchard' from *Custom and Exile* (Allison and Busby, 1985) and 'detente', 'gypsy music in Krakow' from *Hero Dust* (Allison and Busby, 1979).

Elaine Randell for 'Watching Women with Children' from *Beyond All Other* (Pig Press, 1986).

Tom Raworth for 'Horse Power' from *The Mask* (Poltroon, 1976), 'South America' from *Lion Lion* (Trigram Press, 1970), 'Cross Divide' from *Lazy Left Hand* (Actual Size, 1985) and 'Nothing' from *Visible Shivers* (O Books, 1988).

Denise Riley for 'Poor Snow' from *No Fee* (Street Editions, 1977), 'Housing', 'Do So', 'It Really is the Heart' and Virago Press for 'What I Do', 'Affections Must Not' and 'Work' from *Dry Air* (Virago, 1985).

Peter Riley for *Ospita* (Poetical Histories, 1987).

Michèle Roberts and Methuen London for 'Magnificat', 'Rite de Passage' and 'Demeter Grieving' from *The Mirror of the Mother* (Methuen, 1986).

Gavin Selerie for 'Fyllr', 'Garland', 'Poem', 'Paris 1912', 'Exit on Feedback' and 'Azimuth' from *Azimuth* (1984).

Robert Sheppard for 'The Materialisation of Soap 1947' from *The Flashlight Sonata* and a selection from *Letter From the Blackstock Road* (Oasis Books, 1988).

Colin Simms for 'Otter, Redewetter', 'ARCS above OXUS', 'Three Years in Glen Garry' and 'Saint Kilda – Wren, 1957'.

Iain Sinclair for 'Painting with a Knife' and 'Star' from *The Birth Rug* (Albion Village Press, 1973), 'A Bull Called Remorse' and

'German Bite' from *Flesh Eggs & Scalp Metal* (Hoarse Commerce, 1983) and 'Hurricane Drummers' from *Autistic Poses* (Hoarse Commerce, 1985).

Lemn Sissay for 'What Have We Got', 'So Near And Yet So Near' and 'Today Will Pass'.

Ken Smith and Bloodaxe Books Ltd for 'Living with the Boss' and 'Snobby Roberts' Message' from *Terra* (Bloodaxe, 1986), 'The Night Whispers' from *Wormwood* (Bloodaxe, 1987) and the author for 'Jack's Postcards' and 'Writing in Prison'.

Janet Sutherland and The Women's Press for 'Touching heartsease' from *Dancing The Tightrope* (Women's Press, 1987), the author and No Such Press for 'During Long Walks' from *Crossing Over* (No Such, 1983) and the author for 'H ear th'.

Levi Tafari for 'De Tongue' (De First Instrument).

Gael Turnbull and Anvil Press Poetry for 'They Have Taken' and 'Residues: Thronging the Heart' from *A Gathering of Poems 1950-1980* (Anvil Press, 1983).

Michelene Wandor and Journeyman Press for 'Ruth's Story as told to Lilith', 'Eve's Commentary', 'Eve to Lilith' and 'Lilith to Eve' from *Gardens of Eden* (Journeyman Press, 1984).

John Wilkinson for 5 Poems from *Proud Flesh* (Equofinality, 1986).

The general editor wishes to thank Robert Sheppard for fruitful discussions in the early stages of this project; also Patricia Farrell and Gavin Selerie for later suggestions, Tom and Val Raworth for selecting and faxing poems by Asa Benveniste.

■ CONTENTS

xiv

■ BLACK BRITISH POETRY

The cracked lookingglass of a servant James Joyce

A good anthology should hold up a mirror to the area it has chosen
to typify. No mirror could be big enough to take in the entire field
of that activity, therefore whoever is responsible for directing its
aim should be aware of what other mirrors have shown and to
what they have turned a blind eye. It's pointless pretending that
your mirror is the only one around, or the one out to catch the
definitive and best-focused reflection.

This mirror is contemporary, at least. It tries to show off the best
side of its subject, rather than to be a group photo with everyone
crammed in, and each denied hard-won distinguishing features as
a result. The faces it reflects have been around for some time or
will come into their own soon or cannot be ignored, or any
combination of these. They have their equals who are not shown
here, but this is not a head count. It's about a cross-section and
about representation.

For the purposes of this selection Black British has been defined
by residence rather than by possession of a passport. These poets
are distinguished not only by their black identity, though this does
figure as a primary concern in the work of some, but by a strong
sense of being 'other' than what is lauded as indigenous and
capitally British. Their writing tends to argue not just with
themselves and each other, but with society as a whole and their
status in it. Even when the poetry is ostensibly preoccupied with
some other place, it is often instructive as allegory about life in
Britain.

It is becoming increasingly difficult to marginalise a poet on the
basis of his or her racial origin or thematic concerns. This is
perhaps due to a shared commitment to a notion of craft, to being
engaged in an art form which cuts across race and class and shares
a wide and borderless imaginative terrain. However, the realities of
power, of social and economic inequality, do not disappear simply
because a poet makes a bid for the imagination over and above
group or class identity.

Power is as active at the level of poetic discourse as anywhere else, and in this sense Black British poetry reflects a variety of discourses and ideologies. Two black poets in Britain today are likely to have less in common than two poets picked out of a hat. This means that an examination of Black British poetry is at once a scrutiny of what is happening to poetry in Britain as a whole.

Dualisms such as oral and literary, European and African no longer define the work of *individual* poets, much less explain the differences between them. Although some poets are best heard in performance rather than read solely on the page, I would be hard-pressed to confine a poet to one realm or the other. At the level of composition many poets are moving towards a coalition of the two: the performance poem which also works on the page. Poets have often testified to hearing their lines, though they may not be seeing an audience at the time. And those who do write with performance in mind can presume an ever higher level of sophistication in their listeners.

All these poets have a sense of public address, though this may be mediated through an intensely private mask or persona. Their perspective arises out of a particular group experience, but this is not to say that only the groups featured are being addressed. The hope is that this hand-mirror selection will show something of ourselves that is peculiar to us, and by its peculiarity, as human as human can be. In making it I was looking for a true tone and a sense that the poet had wrapped his or her mind around the subject, holding it in a vice-steady grip long enough to reveal something not seen there by us before, something with the spark or steady glow that small truths emit.

Fred D'Aguiar

Listen Mr Oxford Don

Me not no Oxford don
me a simple immigrant
from Clapham Common
I didn't graduate
I immigrate

But listen Mr Oxford don
I'm a man on de run
and a man on de run
is a dangerous one

I ent have no gun
I ent have no knife
but mugging de Queen's English
is the story of my life

I dont need no axe
to split/ up yu syntax
I dont need no hammer
to mash/ up yu grammar

I warning you Mr Oxford don
I'm a wanted man
and a wanted man
is a dangerous one

Dem accuse me of assault
on de Oxford dictionary/
imagine a concise peaceful man like me/
dem want me serve time
for inciting rhyme to riot
but I tekking it quiet
down here in Clapham Common

I'm not a violent man Mr Oxford don
I only armed wit mih human breath
but human breath
is a dangerous weapon

So mek dem send one big word after me
I ent serving no jail sentence
I slashing suffix in self-defence
I bashing future wit present tense
and if necessary

I making de Queen's English accessory/to my offence

Half-caste

Excuse me
standing on one leg
I'm half-caste

Explain yuself
wha yu mean
when yu say half-caste
yu mean when picasso
mix red an green
is a half-caste canvas/
explain yuself
wha yu mean
when yu say half-caste
yu mean when light an shadow
mix in de sky
is a half-caste weather/
well in dat case
england weather
nearly always half-caste
in fact some o dem cloud
half-caste till dem overcast
so spiteful dem dont want de sun pass
ah rass/
explain yuself
wha yu mean
when yu say half-caste
yu mean tchaikovsky
sit down at dah piano
an mix a black key

wid a white key
is a half-caste symphony/

Explain yuself
wha yu mean
Ah listening to yu wid de keen
half of mih ear
Ah lookin at yu wid de keen
half of mih eye
an when I'm introduced to yu
I'm sure you'll understand
why I offer yu half-a-hand
an when I sleep at night
I close half-a-eye
consequently when I dream
I dream half-a-dream
an when moon begin to glow
I half-caste human being
cast half-a-shadow
but yu must come back tomorrow

wid de whole of yu eye
an de whole of yu ear
an de whole of yu mind

an I will tell yu
de other half
of my story

Ghazal

We set our sights on living, and on that alone.
No frenzy – no, no madness must perturb us now.

We'll put no lamp to flicker in the open street
Even the breeze is pledged to side with darkness now

Make sure that no word reaches where it ought to reach
This is a skill the skilful need to practice now.

Loyalty is a myth, and we no longer need
To look for loyal comrades on our journey now.

We homeless wanderers who go from door to door
Find nowhere to lay down our heavy burden now.

We too are much concerned to live a life of ease
Count us with those whom nobody may count on now.

To a Despondent Evening

Strange people, we who trust –
Sad is our fate

That night we should have wakened, that whole night
We passed in dreaming dreams

That name we should have banished from our minds
That name, that single name,
We walked the by-lanes calling out aloud.
That game we should have won we lost repeatedly
Strange people we who trust –
Sad is our fate.

Not one has paid the debt he owed to honour
The bloody hours brought forth no remedy
The years passed by; no miracle occurred
The fire men breathed is quenched

And he who had the bow at his command
Was struck down by the arrow.

The battlements of night await the army of the sun
When will he come for whom all wait?
We who wait, sad is our fate.
Strange people, we who trust.

■ **JAMES BERRY**

Old Man in New Country

I am both Watutsi and Pygmy.
I have shone the moment's glory.
I have been the total loss.

Both leaf and flesh grinder,
both sucker of milk and narcotics,
I have been full and still;
my knees have rattled without flesh.

My shoulder supporting spear and bag,
I have ambled along tracks,
shoeless and not clothed. With leaves,
with secret eyes, with butterflies,
I have been the sun's painting exhibited.

Needing not one machine,
no sounds marked down,
I grew certain with my skills.
From all streams
the seasons wake in my blood.

But challenges and attacks
have entangled my peace.
My bag has repeated emptiness
to my bed. My hands have attended wounds
of wars undeclared.

Now my world is new
I cannot find a waterhole.

Spirits of Movement

Surely, so alike, airborne wind gave birth
to water, issued the denser wash
and earthed the early offspring.

Inbuilt is wind-inheritance.
Rage of leaves resists face-wash
it's wind's arrival in trees.

Hear sea waves work-choir,
hear any waterfall wonder,
it's temple-roar of wind flooding woods.

A restless transparent busyness
going and going. Spirits of movement.
Both break all shores, mad mad in search.

Wind plays wild bands of ghosts.
Water organizes running river
and drives rain-floods hustling.

On any sitting duty
like being a pond or puddle,
canal or glassful

water waits to run away
or just disappear like wind.
In a settled state water is sad.

Drop a stone in a sleepy pool
you hear the sulk
of static water voiced.

Lock up water, give it time, it'll leave.
Drink it down, it presses wanting exit.
A job done, water vanishes.

Water'll freshen any body part
and be ready, hanging
in drips, to be off.

Does its work, yes. But to be
ungraspable, like wind,
water insists on its transfiguration.

New Speaker

I'm the lidded voice from limbo
who can't worry over death
I've long been a ghost
knowing
no more deaths to dread
no more hopes to drain my hope
yet when I make a flame explode
to be commanding bang and fire
as when I throw bricks
and shatter glass
it's because I hope
the crowd will know
and speak my name
as when I smash up shrines
it's my forbidden act
that connects me
with what is sound
and good and wonderful
but can't be shared in peace
and hurting hearts is a balm of hope
in breaking them
like mine has always been
and a hope of release for them
and mine
from barriers
that fix me in pain

Poem for the Wife of an Imprisoned Leader
especially for Winnie Mandela

Defender –
a partner doesn't dance with prison bars.
Denied, a partner dreams up time
when stone does not feel swamped
mixing with air
and earth and water and sunlight

making the fields' blossom-cycles.
    From early times, by stonewalls,
change is an outsider.
Stone knows arrival is final.
    Going and coming
water slips between fingers.
Rock sits out time.
    Doesn't feel. Doesn't see.
Doesn't care. Doesn't walk.,
Stone is unhearing.
Under moon under stars.
Full of sitting years millions.
Dense in self. Where
absence of other levels makes loneliness.
Where distances arrive.
Where time overwhelms for movement.
    Recruits of stone take kingship
in snug walls and signs of walls.
In voices that swagger and declare –
Look how I bulge and drip with excess!
In cries calling calling – Hunger! Hunger!
    Stone-power smashes faces.
Breaks backs like hammered crabs.
Dislodges spines like horsetrampled kittens.
Bashes skulls in like calabashes.
Cracks bones. Chops up breasts.
    The sun returns. The sun piles on
arriving, returning, arriving.
            You a targeted victim
            refuse to be ruled cancelled –
            O what a way you teach.

                Defender –
a partner doesn't swallow stone's
eyeless bulk, doesn't leave
a loved leader walled up.
Stone's reservations' fences mount.
To stone's cold selflove
warmth is a terror.
    Stone calls itself STRONG.

Not opentopped. Not openended.
Nonreceptive. Locked aloof.
Bloodless and guiltless.
Open only for past ages to be resettled.
Unbendable stone stops other voices.
Stops other health.
Bursts bellies of certain babies.
Mangles balls of certain men.
Loosens rocks in thousands
downhill on shacks of bodies.
   Limbs struck off, helplessness works.
Jaws unhinged, speech is snuffed out.
   No courts of law stop stone.
Distress is success.
Tombing is housing.
When – we must arrive and arrive.
Arrival must urge arrival.
   Sunlight becoming avocado and orange,
hypnotic night waves wand of renewal.
         You a targeted victim
         refuse to be ruled cancelled –
         O what a way you teach.

■ VALERIE BLOOM

Longsight Market

Ow much poun fi di yellow yam?
Massa dis tap chat rubbish!
A gole fi yuh yellow yam mek outa
Den ow yuh a sell di saltfish?

Yuh see yuh, Hell naw miss yuh
For yuh too wretched tief.
Put i back, mi no millionaire.
Mek ahsee dah tin a corn beef.

Wait, a from when dem yah sinting deh yah?
Mussa from di year a nought!
Meck has'e teck i, oh yuh hab red peas,
Meck ah see't, a oomuch a quart?

Tap, ow yuh wan get rich quick soh,
Yuh noh fraid yuh go a jail?
Yuh cyan get six mont fi robbery yuh know.
What a poun fi yuh pigtail?

Yuh cussid face faba eighty pence
Move yuhsef – but koo yah lawd!
Koo di plantain whey di man a sell
Yuh noh shame fi cyah dis from yahd?

Dem deh wi gi smaddy consumption
Dem nat even fit fi hag.
Shet yuh mout, noh badda rush mi,
Yuh hab brown rice? Oomuch a bag?

Dat noh too bad, meck ah see't.
No massa, dis too dutty,
Gimme half a dah bun deh, but see yah
Ow yuh mean yuh cyaan cut i?

Lissen man, dis shet yuh mout yah
Nobody noh hurry mi,
Mi haffe meck sure mi get good tings
For mi wuk too hard fi mi two quatty.

People a wait noh? Meck dem tan deh
Dis gi mi one bag a toto,
(Dem yah green banana look sick sah)
An beg yuh pass mi one cho-cho.

What a mango dem fubba-fubba,
Oonu wont sell tings force-ripe?
Look ow di pitata dem twis up-twis up
Lacka when jackass hab gripe

Aright, dat wi do fi teday
Ow yuh mean ef dat is all?
Dat is all yes – tap, wait one minute
Meck ahsee dat tin o milo by di wall.

Eh eh, mi see't, now put i back
Add up di mi now, dis an dat,
Yuh cyan tan deh ax fi one poun
For a fifty pence mi gat.

Well yuh should'n sell soh dear,
Tap likkle, but yuh noh hab noh corn?
An mi ben wan' two corn fi buy yuh know,
Mi wi gi yuh di balance nex week, mi gawn.

Riddym Ravings (The Mad Woman's Poem)

De fus time dem kar me go a Bellevue was fi di dactar an de
   lanlord operate
and tek de radio out a mi head,
troo dem seize de bed
weh did a gimme cancer
an mek mi talk to nobady
Ah di same night wen dem trow mi out fe no pay de rent
mi haffi sleep outadoor wid de Channel One riddym box
an de D.J. fly up eena mi head
mi hear im a play seh

Eh, Eh,
No feel no way
Town is a place dat ah really kean stay
Dem kudda – ribbit mi han
Eh – ribbit mi toe
Mi waan go a country go look mango

Fah wen hungry mek king street pavement bubble an dally
in front a mi yeye,
An mi foot start wanda falla fly
to de garbage pan eena de Chinaman backlat
dem nearly chap aff mi han eena de butcha shap
fi de piece a ratten poke
ah de same time de mawga gal in front a mi
drap de laas piece a ripe banana
an MI – ben dung – pick i' up – an nyam i'
a dat time dem grab mi an kar mi back a Bellevue
Dis time de dactar an de lanlord aperate
an tek de radio plug out a mi head
dem sen mi out, seh mi alright
but
as ah ketch back out a street
ah push een back de plug – hear mi DJ a play, seh

17

Eh, Eh
No feel no way
Town is a place dat ah really kean stay
Dem kudda – ribbit mi han
Eh – ribbit mi toe
Mi waan go a country go look mango

Ha Haah . . . Haa

Wen mi fus come a town
mi use to tell everey bady 'mawnin'
but as de likkle rosiness gawn outa mi face
nobady nah ansa mi
silence tun rags roun mi bady in de midst a all de dead people dem
a bawl bout de caast of livin'
an a ongle one ting tap me fram go stark ravin mad
a wer mi siddung eena Parade
a tear up newspaper fi talk to
an sometime dem roll up
an tun eena one a Uncle But sweet saaf yellow heart breadfruit
wid piece a roas saalfish side a i'
an if likkle rain jus fall
me get cocanat rundung fe eat i' wid
same place side a weh di country bus dem pull out
an sometime mi a try board de bus
an di canductar bwoy a halla out seh,
'Dutty gal, kum affa di bus'
Ah troo im noh hear di riddym eena mi head
same as de tape weh di bus driva a play, seh

Eh, Eh
No feel no way
Town is a place dat ah really kean stay
Dem kudda – ribbit mi han
Eh – ribbit mi toe
Mi waan go a country go look mango
So country bus, ah beg yuh
tek mi home
to de place, where I belang . . .

an di dutty bway jus run mi aff

Well dis mawnin, mi start out pon Spanish Town Road,
fah mi deh go walk go home a country

fah my gramma use to tell mi how she walk from Wes
come a town
come sell food
an mi waan ketch home befo' dem put de price pan i'
But mi kean go home dutty?
fah mi parents dem did sen mi out clean
Ai!
see wan stanpipe deh!
so mi strip aff all de crocus bag dem
an scrub unda mi armpit
fah mi hear di two mawga gal dem laas nite a laugh
an seh
'Who kudda breed smaddy like me?'
A troo dem no know seh a pure nice man
weh drive car
an have gun
visit my piazza all dem four a' clack a mawnin
no de likkle dutty bway dem when mi see dem a go home wid
But as ah feel de clear water pon mi bady
no grab dem grab mi
an is back eena Bellevue dem kar mi
seh me mad an a bade naked pon street
Well dis time de dactar an de lanlord operate
an dem tek di whole radio from outa mi head
but wen dem tink seh mi unda chlorofarm
dem put i' dung careless
an when dem gawn
mi tek di radio – an mi push i' up eena mi belly
fi keep de baby company
far even if mi noh mek i'
Me waan my baby know dis yah riddym yah
fram befo she bawn
Hear de DJ a play, seh

Eh, Eh
No feel no way
Town is a place dat ah really kean stay
Dem kudda – ribbit mi han
Eh – ribbit mi toe
Mi waan go a country go look mango

An same time
de dactar an de lanlord
tigger de electric shack
an mi hear de DJ vice bawl out, seh
'MURTHER'.
                    PULL UP MISSA OPERATOR!

Omens of the Morning

1
PROPHET
Nostradamus returns
In a prophecy of the New World;
His space-ship, Survivor
Streams through an omen of the morning
And through an April dooryard,
A fire still burns.

Was this history's wrong turning,
The yearning of the distant dead
Drowned in the river of separation?

Entering the calling world
He had echoed, umbilical
Coming home, calling
In the time-slip of the conqueror.

He draws a line
With the dawn
In the centre of the earth
Where the sky would fall
Into pieces of Mars,
And on the sons of stars,
A sign
Of the Creator is worn.

Earth-music fills the seeds
Giving birth
To gardens over the Atlantic;
Nostradamus rhymes the blood,
Glittering green
In the ripe flowers of his eyes
Reflecting neon.
In the cities' never-ending mirth,
Every sky-scraper is a dinosaur

Chasing its own image in a mirage
Mirroring mammon.

The morning ripens
With the grammar of machines,
Driving a dream in the roots of stars
Sky-writing on new faces.
Nostradamus rolls out a vision
Of the tropics turning cold
When rockets blast,
Casting wintry shadows
On the young, bright spur of youth;
But beyond the sky-ward abode
Of poets,
The morning cockerel sings deliverance.

After the blazing blue of eyes,
The four-seasoned beaten cries,
The cold sun ascending in the morning,
White skin invisible in pink,
The ship from the colonies, survives;
Inside the snowed carcass of a man,
Light is growing
And Nostradamus sows remembered hot roots
Of the survivor imagining home.

■ **MERLE COLLINS**

Callaloo*

Mix up
like callaloo
Not no watery callaloo
But
a thick, hot, sweet
callaloo
burnin' you tongue
Wid dem chunk o' dumplin'
goin' down nice
an' wid coconut
wid o' widdout deaders
as de case may be
as de taste may be
as de pocket may be
but sweet
an' hot

Dat is what it feel like
to be part o' dis
Revolution reality
O' dis
wakin' up reality
o' dis
no more hidin' you passport
reality
no more
hangin' you head
an' shufflin' you foot
an' tryin' to hide
behin' de person
in front o' you
like little Janet
behin' she mudder skirt

* *Popular soup made from the leaf of the dasheen plant*

when de man ask
'whey you from?'

No more
playin' you doh hear
or sayin' some shit like
A . . . a . . . a . . . island
near by Trinidad
Or
a . . . a few mile
off Venezuela
but out loud an' bole
like you make de name
GRENADA!

An' wid you head in de air
becus de world is yours
an' you know is yours
an' you not goin' be
meek
meek
meek
an' wait to see
if
somebody
goin' let you
inherit the earth
becus you know arready
is yours

so you say
loud
an' clear
an' proud
GRENADA!
an' you silent scream
which he musbe hear
becus he look up
into your claimin' eyes
says
Dat mean Revolution

Dat mean Progress
Dat mean Forward!
Dat mean
sharin'
an' carin'
an' believin'
an' livin'
an' lovin'

Dat mean
a country in the Caribbean
in Latin America
in the Americas
in the struggle
in the world

Dat mean, Comrade
a people
like de people
in Cuba
in Nicaragua
In Zimbabwe
in Mozambique
in strugglin' South Africa
in all dem countries
whey de people know
dat doh donkey say
de worl' ain't level
even donkey heself
musbe does shake he head
to feel dem bumps
an' know

how t'ing so hard
for some toe
an' so sof'
for others

All o' we
in all o' dis worl'
so mix up
like callaloo

an' yet
so not like callaloo
an' dat is why
de change
an' de promise
of de change
is sweet an' strong

like de soup
w'en Grannie
cover it down dey
an' let it
consomme
like dat
hot
sweet
burnin'
heavy
heavy

ca-lla-loo !

Coolie Odyssey
for Ma, d. 1985

Now that peasantry is in vogue,
Poetry bubbles from peat bogs,
People strain for the old folk's fatal gobs
Coughed up in grates North or North East
'Tween bouts o' livin dialect,
It should be time to hymn your own wreck,
Your house the source of ancient song:
Dry coconut shells cackling in the fireside
Smoking up our children's eyes and lungs,
Plantains spitting oil from a clay pot,
Thick sugary black tea gulped down.

The calves hustle to suck,
Bawling on their rope but are beaten back
Until the cow is milked.
Frantic children call to be fed.
Roopram the Idiot goes to graze his father's goats backdam
Dreaming that the twig he chews so viciously in his mouth
Is not a twig.

In a winter of England's scorn
We huddle together memories, hoard them from
The opulence of our masters.

You were always back home, forever
As canefield and whiplash, unchanging
As the tombstones in the old Dutch plot
Which the boys used for wickets playing ball.

Over here Harilall who regularly dodged his duties at the
    marketstall
To spin bowl for us in the style of Ramadhin
And afterwards took his beating from you heroically
In the style of England losing
Is now known as the local Paki
Doing slow trade in his Balham cornershop.

Is it because his heart is not in business
But in the tumble of wickets long ago
To the roar of wayward boys?
Or is it because he spends too much time
Being chirpy with his customers, greeting
The tight-wrapped pensioners stalking the snow
With tropical smile, jolly small chat, credit?
They like Harilall, these muted claws of Empire,
They feel privileged by his grinning service,
They hear steelband in his voice
And the freeness of the sea.
The sun beams from his teeth.

Heaped up beside you Old Dabydeen
Who on Albion Estate clean dawn
Washed obsessively by the canal bank,
Spread flowers on the snake-infested water,
Fed the gods the food that Chandra cooked,
Bathed his tongue of the creole
Babbled by low-caste infected coolies.
His Hindi chants terrorized the watertoads
Flopping to the protection of bush.
He called upon Lord Krishna to preserve
The virginity of his daughters
From the Negroes,
Prayed that the white man would honour
The end-of-season bonus to Poonai
The canecutter, his strong, only son:
Chandra's womb being cursed by deities
Like the blasted land
Unconquerable jungle or weed
That dragged the might of years from a man.
Chandra like a deaf-mute moved about the house
To his command,
A fearful bride barely come-of-age
Year upon year swelling with female child.
Guilt clenched her mouth
Smothered the cry of bursting apart:
Wrapped hurriedly in a bundle of midwife's cloth
The burden was removed to her mother's safekeeping.

He stamped and cursed and beat till he turned old
With the labour of chopping tree, minding cow, building fence
And the expense of his daughters' dowries.
Dreaming of India
He drank rum
Till he dropped dead
And was buried to the singing of Scottish Presbyterian hymns
And a hell-fire sermon from a pop-eyed bawling catechist,
By Poonai, lately baptized, like half the village.

Ever so old,
Dabydeen's wife,
Hobbling her way to fowl-pen,
Cussing low, chewing her cud, and lapsed in dream,
Sprinkling rice from her shrivelled hand.
Ever so old and bountiful,
Past where Dabydeen lazed in his mudgrave,
Idle as usual in the sun,
Who would dip his hand in a bowl of dhall and rice –
Nasty man, squelching and swallowing like a low-caste sow –
The bitch dead now!

The first boat chugged to the muddy port
Of King George's Town. Coolies come to rest
In El Dorado,
Their faces and best saries black with soot.
The men smelt of saltwater mixed with rum.
The odyssey was plank between river and land,
Mere yards but months of plotting
In the packed bowel of a white man's boat
The years of promise, years of expanse.
At first the gleam of the green land and the white folk and the
    Negroes,
The earth streaked with colour like a toucan's beak,
Kiskidees flame across a fortunate sky,
Canefields ripening in the sun
Wait to be gathered in armfuls of gold.

I have come back late and missed the funeral.
You will understand the connections were difficult.
Three airplanes boarded and many changes
Of machines and landscapes like reincarnations

To bring me to this library of graves,
This small clearing of scrubland.
There are no headstones, epitaphs, dates.
The ancestors curl and dry to scrolls of parchment.
They lie like texts
Waiting to be written by the children
For whom they hacked and ploughed and saved
To send to faraway schools.
Is foolishness fill your head.
Me dead.
Dog-bone and dry-well
Got no story to tell.
Just how me born stupid is so me gone.
Still we persist before the grave
Seeking fables.
We plunder for the maps of El Dorado
To make bountiful our minds in an England
Starved of gold.

Albion village sleeps, hacked
Out between bush and spiteful lip of river.
Folk that know bone
Fatten themselves on dreams
For the survival of days.
Mosquitoes sing at a nipple of blood.
A green-eyed moon watches
The rheumatic agony of houses crutched up on stilts
Pecked about by huge beaks of wind,
That bear the scars of ancient storms.
Crappeau clear their throats in hideous serenade,
Candleflies burst into suicidal flame.
In a green night with promise of rain
You die.

We mark your memory in songs
Fleshed in the emptiness of folk,
Poems that scrape bowl and bone
In English basements far from home,
Or confess the lust of beasts
In rare conceits
To congregations of the educated

Sipping wine, attentive between courses –
See the applause fluttering from their white hands
Like so many messy table napkins.

Coolie Mother

Jasmattie live in bruk –
Down hut big like Bata shoe-box,
Beat clothes, weed yard, chop wood, feed fowl
For this body and that body and every blasted body,
Fetch water, all day fetch water like if the whole –
Whole slow-flowing Canje river God create
Just for *she* one own bucket.

Till she foot-bottom crack and she hand cut-up
And curse swarm from she mouth like red-ants
And she cough blood on the ground but mash it in:
Because Jasmattie heart hard, she mind set hard

To hustle save she one-one slow penny,
Because one-one dutty make dam cross the Canje
And she son Harilall *got* to go school in Georgetown,
Must wear clean starch pants, or they go laugh at he,
Strap leather on he foot, and he *must* read book,
Learn talk proper, take exam, go to England university,
Not turn out like he rum-sucker chamar* dadee.

* 'chamar' – low-caste

Rotogravure

From the scripture
From the radiocarbon lab
O silent God
Hear us good Lord.
Beginning with a postscript
The tinsel bragadoccio of oppression
Voices from within the veil
The rule of reason, death and war
The shadow of years born
By a golden river: origin
As the son of a revolt, become
Reconciled with a strange land

The archivist saw into the past
And future by a delicacy of reading
Perusing the trace. He concludes:
'Around 1787;
Of her many sons
And one Othello of the woods'.
Re-assembling what he called
The blossom of revolt
To form a patchwork, he says
Quite snug there in history:
It is yours to keep.
His pen is time

It was he who wrote, traced
On her luckily brownskinned body
Descended of fine slaves.
Spinning pages of fictional memory
Originating a desire
At the scene of consciousness
He would root me with an unbroken line
The sum of my presence
The rebel having forgotten himself
Born with a flood

Running Dutch French Spanish blood
But hooray no Anglo Saxon!
He is reprieved from degeneration.

But many copies can be produced
The rotograph will only repeat
Allowing the manuscript infinity
And the joy of duplication
Will still the spora of linneage
Onto an image. He said
Ours is the second miracle age.
He never raised his hat
To a white woman again

from **Fragments of the Green Island**

Ah! die to childhood. let the poem die the syntax
fall apart. let all the inessential words be swallowed up.
The weight of the rhythm is enough. no need of
word cement to build on the rock of the city of tomorrow.
(Leopold Sedar Senghor)

1
If only
Under the canopy of stars
The humid blanket of night
One small whisper moving
Northward to the mountains

Summon the promontory of days
Reduced to little droplets
On the still surface of the future

Here and now
I am in a tropical storm
The leaves tremble a little
Suggesting approaching rain
Or change

If only
Drenched in a cascade of desire
The island became itself
Once again

3

The tangerine sky is hopeful
Hollow mercy of this amber basin
Walled in by the green colossi
And the valley is full of gold

I am ashamed of you
All resplendent in puffballs of bamboo
Your feet are scorched by the red lake
And your bass voice is muffled by ferns

Mad-voiced chunter
In cackles fluttering up to the treetops
Rising up to the blue-grey heights
The mountains are full of dreams
The bright outer contours of desire
Glimpsing itself in the future

The driver's machismo bucks the bus
Like a stallion over the impossible hill road
Up past the frowzy air of downtown
Zigzagging up to scented driveways

Bourgeois houses cling precariously
To the exclusive uptown rocks
Like rumours of decline
And rumours of progress

This hot and sullen peace
Whose night engulfs the hillside
As the voice of a young preacher
Rises and falls in growls and whispers

Above the howling litany of dogs
Prophets and serpents coil themselves
On the silent barb of the night
Shrouding the island's misery in music

For the cars of the dead martyrs
They sing a paradiso
In glory to Him who moves all things
Who penetrates this cusp of stars

Flying Home

The sky's blue lapels flap open,
the cloud makes a fine herring-bone fossil.

I am an Englishman motoring to the airport
for my mother's funeral. Time was

she would press a leaf-skeleton,
a white carnation to my button-hole –

her purple hat blowing like a rose
with the scent of moth-balls and net-curtains

at her window. The plane lifts off:
looking down on stills of fields, hangars, houses,

mother, I am flying!

From No Blacks, No Irish
Scene 6 The Boat Passage

BOYO: When I came to this country, I could
have flown. It's cheaper by boat. The money
I saved showed me Casablanca, Lisbon, Bordeaux:
slowly into Europe. There is no shadow in
Europe, everything is exposed to snow: the
cafes in France, chairs and tables in orderly
rows, and snow falling gently on the upholstery.
When they spoke English, it felt like coming
home. Southampton, game-reserve of the
industrial English: long, loose cranes looming
their curious shapes into our hull. On the
quayside, a few crates, the six passengers
dumping their cases in snow. And English
people: it seemed they might shake off the
cold snow at any moment, and call out to ask

us where we'd been. No-one spoke. Our breath
frosted as we stood there, looking at England.

Padraic's Point

A few, wild handfuls of rock
flung out to sea from Scotland,
they have rooted, these Hebrides,
in waters treacherous with flux
and history.
                    In cross-currents
of the cold Atlantic seaboard –
theirs the mystic's compass
of God and mists – men fought
with coils of its heaving bulk,
the slattering rain, the long
tonsured, floundering wave, on
boards whose scuttled hulks
have sunk like days below
the world's wet rim.
                    Now,
under dark furls of the cloud,
light-bursts shift along
the western corridor of light,
illumine crinkled, parchment seas
and point this cowl-grey, granite
beak of rock to wind-wrung journeys –
as Viking, Gael and Spaniard
saw new worlds within the reach
of longboat, coracle and galley.

Only a play of storm-light,
closing out history, echoes
down the dull, grey, trenchant surge
to meet here on this rock,
a sounding stone above the murmur.

The Sewing-Box
for Rita Gbadamosi

Undoing the straps,
the soft leather fetishes
along the wicker rim,

lifting the box
onto my lap, like a cat,
and running my finger

under the lid –
solid, irregular, strange –
the box stirred.

Opened, the shock
of your life
tumbled out: pins, needles,

coloured thread,
reels, odd recipes,
your notes going back

before my birth –
a diary in miniature –
scissors, hair clips,

an old bone brooch,
'fifties dress patterns
sutured to the hip.

The seed-packet
I found and opened
has let such florid,

purple flowers out.
A late blossoming
at your hands and feet.

Mediatrix

1 Zone

Camera angles. Drear lighting.
Compound. Images of our lives

Brutalised by the garbage,
The rotten. Street defiled.

This is your life, our
Lives. Caught through a lens

TV screens, there is no hope
No colour no life, utter despair.

Inner/outer, complete
A perpetual autumn, ghetto decay.

This, our lives through eyes
Atrophied vision.

A balanced viewpoint, to reflect
On. A theme. Societal. Deprivation

London. Style: Blacklife, style.

2 I and I

The subject is full in his
Power, lying prone, ready
For attack

The subject is ready, electric
Behind the funk, wide
Eyed. A wild Jonathan

A blade in the eye
Of the lens, claiming power

The subject is power, us
Blacks. And always desired
As other

3 Refugees and Pirates

A guitar in the shape of Africa.

First the good news. On the edge
Popping champagne corks
Harare
And no rain is due.
The green revolution remains incipient.

And where it's getting worse
The geography,
The map,
In the Sahel.
Broken, the emergency remains

Exodus.
The law of the return
Unlike the Entebbe raid
They stumble, barefoot from the plane
Clutching cans
Are we really in Zion?

Ashklon.
A dramatic leap in time
They are taught the basics
Pushing a switch

Naked, except for a T-shirt
Israel is beset.
Brought in like thieves in the night
They are obliged to undergo ritual
Immersion.

Twelve Third World countries have rejected free powdered milk and
butter donated by the EEC, because of fears of radio-active contamination
from the Chernobyl accident.
(The Guardian   8 March 1988)

Recollections of the Sun

I walk through sunlit gardens
noting the exhilaration of bodies:
women posed in careless flesh,
young men arching deep muscles to this heat;

suddenly I recollect
totally dependent eyes squinting at the nipple.

It must have been at dawn then
that I began to notice it.

I believed that the Sun
was there to bring adventure,
to make jewels happen in the grass
which grew only for feet to trample over;

I believed there was nothing cleverer than people,
for gods, enchantresses,
remained where they belong,
trapped in paper
lived there unhappily ever after,
but people were awake
and really ate.

By midmorning I ate endlessly
making want different from need;
I was a Giant.

Even noon though hot and sweaty
was in my power,
dark was unbelievable,
the diamond river tonned with manoeuvrable shipping
I captaining an ocean-goer
carrying me sound and prosperous
beyond hazards of horizons.

(Soundless moves the great ship
In green unfathomed waters.)

It was very close to evening
when clouds come stumbling stupidly
and the ways seemed pressingly to narrow
(sudden rocks throwing curious reflections)
when pilots pointed wildly to the shore
asking variable questions
that I thought about a safe mooring.

Late, I climbed unfamiliar mountains
where cold began possessively to tighten.
I was glad to have reachable companions
but not very many,
glad the luggage I was carrying
was hardly necessary,
I was getting out of breath,
the long journey weary in the bone.

Stopped in a peculiar silence
I turned toward the sky
(the ground was waterless and split,
trees arrogant and barren).
I noticed then the Sun was flying away,
a Carnival balloon I once had
but lost hold of
never knowing how;

I wanted to give back everything,
to be able to make it stay,
stop it from ever disappearing . . .

Dark is unbelievable.
I am quite alone.
I wonder if I am certain there is ever going to be a new day.

Deflowering

Winter trees thrown upwards,
sprinkling the air with branches;
sometimes the window sunless,
sometimes night creeping in.

Inside,
candles, hearts that melt,
photographs, smells,
hair on pillow,

dreams, paperflesh,
manacled syllables, imprisoned blood;
the whisper of word,
sigh of line.

In the morning,
inkstains on the sheet.

Work-in-progress

1
They crawled out slowly
from their caves,
silver spiders.
The night held them
static in its net
of black jelly.
When the earth turned
                          the sun
melted the night's blackness.
the stars fell over
the edge
          and we were freed
from our enslavement.

2

The stars came out
one night without
their faces.
They had no eyes
nor spoke to us
through their dark lips.
A crippled shadow
wept over the clouds
where the moon might have been.
They said in the village
that a woman lost her child.
When the sun came out
we discovered the unity

of faceless dreamers.

3

Nobody thought
that it could be so small, so ugly
When the star fell,
all eyes turned upwards.
Its silver signature
tore the darkness.
A visual scream
in the silence of night.
When they found the star
they could not believe it.

4

It was the black
star
in the white sky.
Shining in its brilliance.
It was the shadow of the sun
but at night
it became all space.
The night belonged
to the black star
but the silver stars

stood out smiling.
They did not know
how many had lost their way
in the laughter
of the black star.

The Identikit

I have broken step and faith
with the agony of a smile
which fits

On a street in Roseau
the laugh
a gesture
Without a second thought
I claimed them

The walk
identical to his
was saved from an
early morning
Castries rain

I held the eyes
on a crowded bus to Port-of-Spain
They glanced into my own
I would not
let them go.

I found the hands
on Grand Anse beach
They brushed my own
I kept the touch

Preoccupation with
obsessive love
It fills the void
the dreams of hollow
substance

Drawn in indelible lines
etched with longing
the image must be precise
It is taking time

but I will get there
in the end

Conqueror of a Forbidden Landscape

   He was lost

Leroy was lost before he began

Valley of mysterious promise

Closed his eyes
to walk the petal soft
perfumed way

Edged his way in torment
he may lose life and limb

Perilous journey

Kept his balance
                        dangerous
                                    taut

Straining to rise
and fall with each inclination
lifted himself with the impetus

He would get to the other side
in time
in time to straddle
and conquer

but for now
                    he teetered on the brink
trembling

Beads of perspiration softened any sharpness
melting defined line which glistened
against a velvet black

Hills

Valley of mysterious promise

He could bask along the stream
keep himself cool
shelter and be lost
inside the caves

Slide into a curve

Boy, yuh ehn hah no shame?!!

slide to

Miss Millie!

slip further

Yes Miss Agnes!

deeper into

Is so you bringin' up yuh son?

the sweet

De boy eyein' up meh tut-tuts

gentle

Leroy!

waters

How he get to be so dam' fresh-up?

where no

boy is cut-arse fuh yuh

one could reach
him

He loved her
    loved Miss Agnes
through sleepless nights
haunted classroom hours
tortured tongue-tied indecision
to offer his feelings

    loved since crouching low
among bamboo he had watched
                    watched until there was nothing
            to see

What was pain compared
with the triumph he felt
then and was feeling
now?

Reggae fi Dada

galang dada
galang gwaan yaw sah
yu nevah ad noh life fi live
jus di wan life fi give
yu did yu time pan ert
yu nevah get yu just dizert
galang goh smile inna di sun
galang goh smile inna di sun
galang goh satta inna di palace af peace

o di waatah
it soh deep
di waatah
it soh daak
an it full a hawbah shaak

di lan is like a rack
slowly shattahrin to san
sinkin in a sea of calamity
where fear breeds shadows
dat lurk in di daak
where people fraid fi waak
fraid fi tink fraid fi taak
where di present is haunted by di paas

a deh soh mi bawn
get fi know bout staam
learn fi cling to di dawn
an wen mi hear mi daddy sick
mi quickly pack mi grip an tek a trip

mi nevah have noh time
wen mi reach
fi si noh sunny beach
wen mi reach
jus people a live in shack
people livin back-to-back

mongst cackroach an rat
mongst dirt an dizeez
subjek to terrorist attack
political intrigue
kanstant grief
an noh sign af relief

o di grass
turn brown
soh many trees
cut doun
an di lan is ovahgrown
fram country to town
is jus thistle an tawn
inna di woun a di poor
is a miracle ow dem endure

di pain nite an day
di stench of decay
di glarin sights
di guarded affluence
di arrogant vices
cole eyes of kantemp
di mackin symbals of independence

a deh soh mi bawn
get fi know bout staam
learn fi clin to di dawn
an wen di news reach mi
seh mi wan daddy ded
mi ketch a plane quick

an wen mi reach mi sunny isle
it woz di same ole style
di money well dry
di bullits dem a fly
plenty innocent a die
many rivahs run dry
ganja plane flyin high
di poor man im a try
yu tink a lickle try im try
holdin awn bye an bye

wen a dallah cant buy
a lickle dinnah fi a fly

galang dada
galang gwaan yaw sah
yu nevah ad noh life fi live
just di wan life fi give
yu did yu time pan ert
yu nevah get yu jus dizert
galang goh smile inna di sun
galang goh satta inna di palace af peace

mi know you couldn tek it dada
di anguish an di pain
di suffahrin di prablems di strain
di strugglin in vain
fi mek two ens meet
soh dat dem pickney coulda get
a lickle someting fi eat
fi put cloaz pan dem back
fi put shoes pan dem feet
wen a dallah cant buy
a lickle dinnah fi a fly

mi know yu try dada
yu fite a good fite
but di dice dem did loaded
an di card pack fix
yet still yu reach fifty-six
before yu lose yu leg wicket
'a noh yu bawn grung here'
soh wi bury yu a Stranger's Burying Groun
near to mhum an cousin Daris
nat far fram di quarry
doun a August Town

Baby Lazarus

When I got home

I went out into the garden
liking it when the frost bit
my old brown boots
and dug a hole the size of a baby
and buried the clothes
I'd bought anyway, just in case.

A week later I stood at my window
and saw the ground move
and swell the promise of a crop;
that's when she started crying.

I gave her a service then
sang Ye Banks And Braes
planted a bush of roses
read from the Bible, the book of Job
cursed myself digging a pit for my baby
sprinkling ash from the grate.

Late that same night
she came in by the window
my baby Lazarus
and suckled at my breast.

That Distance Apart

I am only nineteen
my whole life is changing

tonight I see her
shuttered eyes in my dreams

I cannot pretend she's never been
my stitches pull and threaten to snap

my own body a witness
leaking blood to sheets milk to shirts

my stretch marks
record that birth

though I feel like somebody is dying

I stand up in my bed
and wail like a banshee

II

On the second night
I shall suffocate her with a feather pillow

bury her under a weeping willow
or take her far out to sea

and watch her tiny six pound body
sink to shells and re shape herself

so much better than her body
encased in glass like a museum piece

Or I shall stab myself
cut my wrists   steal some sleeping pills

better than this – mummified
preserved as a warning

III

On the third night I toss
I did not go through those months

for you to die on me now
on the third night I lie

willing life into her
breathing air all the way down the corridor

to the glass cot
I push my nipples through

feel the ferocity of her lips

IV

Here
landed in a place I recognize

my eyes in the mirror
hard marbles glinting

murderous light
my breasts sag   my stomach

still soft as a baby's
my voice deep and old as ammonite

I am a stranger visiting
myself occasionally

an empty ruinous house
cobwebs dust and broken stairs

inside woodworm
outside the weeds grow   tall

as she must be now

V

She, my little foreigner
no longer familiar with my womb

kicking her language of living
somewhere past stalking her first words

she is six years old today
I am twenty-five; we are only

that distance apart yet
time has fossilised

prehistoric time is easier
I can imagine dinosaurs

more vivid than my daughter
dinosaurs do not hurt my eyes

nor make me old so terribly old
we are land sliced and torn.

The Mother Poem (two)

I always wanted to give birth
do that incredible natural thing
that women do – I nearly broke down
when I heard we couldn't
and then my man said to me
well there's always adoption
(we didn't have test tubes and the rest
then) and well even in the early sixties there was something
scandalous about adopting
telling the world your secret failure
bringing up an alien child
who knew what it would turn out to be?

but I wanted a baby badly
didn't need to come from my womb
or his seed for me to love it did it
and I had sisters who looked like me
didn't need carbon copy features
blueprints for generations
it was a baby a baby   a baby I wanted

so I watched my child grow
always the first to hear her in the night
all this umbilical knot business   is
nonsense – the men can afford deeper sleeps
that's all. I listened to hear her talk
and when she did I heard my voice under hers
and now some of her mannerisms
crack me up

all them stories could have really had me
believing unless you are breast fed
you'll never be close and the rest
my daughter's warmth spills over me
leaves a gap
when she's gone
I think of her mother. She remembers how I read her
all those newspaper and magazine
cuttings about adoption

she says her head's an encyclopedia
of sob stories: the ones that were never
told and committed suicide on their wedding nights

I always believed in the telling anyhow
you can't keep something like that secret
I wanted her to think of her other mother
out there thinking that child I had will be
eight today nine today all the way up to
god knows when. I told my daughter;
I bet your mother's never missed your birthday
how could she

now when people say ah but
it's not like having your own child though is it
I say of course it is what else is it
she's my child I have brought her up
told her stories wept at losses
laughed at her pleasures she is mine.

yes. Well maybe that is why I don't
like all this talk about her being black
I brought her up as my own
as I would any other child
colour matters to the nutters
but she says my daughter says
it matters to her.

I suppose there would have been things
I couldn't understand with any child
we knew she was coloured
they told us they had no babies at first
and I chanced to say it didn't matter
what colour it was and then they
said oh well are you sure in that case
we have a baby for you
to think she wasn't even thought of as a baby!
my baby my baby.

Lure of the Cascadura

Exiled under silver birch and conifers
I see the poui and immortelles blooming;

the mistle-thrush sings,
but I hear the kiskadee,
                    'Qu'est ce qu'il dit,
                    qu'est ce qu'il dit.'

Blue crabs scuttle in mangrove mud
where this forest floor is a compost
of dead leaves;

that grey squirrel is no agouti
sniffing the air for hunters in rain forest;

I listen to the birch's sigh
and hear distant rain approaching;

pewah and pomme-arac
usurp the taste of peach and Cox's pippin;

but I have savoured the cascadura
spiced with legend and must return to die
where the scarlet ibis flame.

'Skin Skin, Yuh Na Know Meh'

Soucouyant, Soucouyant,
ball of fire vampiring through the night,
I found your skin beneath a water barrel
                    and salted it,
                    and salted it;

'Skin skin, is me, yuh na know meh,
skin skin, yuh na know meh'.

No more banquets of blood,
no more purple rings
on my skin in the mornings;
no more chalk marks: crosses and noughts
on doors and windows to keep you away;
I found your skin beneath a water barrel
and salted it,
and salted it;

'Skin skin, is me, yuh na know meh,
skin skin, yuh na know meh'.

In daylight, you, an old woman leaning on stick,
shunned the chalk line across your path;
you raved and cursed
marking your next victim with blaze of your eyes.
Children taunted you:
'Soucouyant, Soucouyant !'
But I found your skin beneath a water barrel
and salted it,
and salted it;

'Skin skin, is me, yuh na know meh,
skin skin, yuh na know meh'.

Island Muse

I come with my pen
from Baptist Shouters,
candles burning on the edge of darkness,
at the side of the road in limbo,
where repentance sings
in hallelujahs,
in amens,
in the clapping harmony of hymns.

I come with my pen
from the drum, drum
drumming Shango rhythms
in the tent of dancing sacrifices,
in the pulsing blood squirts of cocks' hearts.
From the drum, drum
drumming on calabash-covered chicken,
drumming away death with Yoruba magic.

I come with my pen
walking the middle of the jumbie midnight road,
hair standing up, heart big in mouth,
clinging to 'our Fathers', 'Lord is my Shepherds',
avoiding dubious pools,
avoiding obeah big foot,
smelling cacajab,
walking backwards through front door.

I come with my pen
from where the jumbie 'buds' at midday
hoot, hoot, hoot from the sandbox tree
and the dog-wailing, death-song
suck the last breath of the ailing;
crapaud hopping into drawing room,
mirrors cracking suddenly,
wind coming from nowhere
blows out pitchoil lamps
and blessed candles.

I come with my pen
from cool green forest
where Papa Bois, bearded with vines,
protects the gouti, lapp and quenk;
where macajuel, like fallen-down tree trunk,
sleeps with belly full of cow.
Where mapepire zanana strikes
the deer-chasing dog,
while cigals trill for rain.

I come with my pen
from the wily douens,
kidnappers of kiddies under full moon,
faceless, walking forward, backwards into bush;

from where Mama maladé is a naked baby
under midnight street lamp whimpering,
La Diablesse hiding her cow foot
under wide french petticoat,
Soucouyant and loupgarou, balls of fire,
brightening roof tops before the sucking feasts.

I come long years with my pen
and island hauntings
from where my navel string tree
still grows.

Towards the End of a Century

i

My hand is steady:
This, my friends, is no mannerism
From an adopted land. A mother's mother
Instructed us: *Do not grow old*
In a place unkind to you. This brought
Me back. The hand
Is no reek of manliness,
More the hint of some little way to go
Before the words serve their sentence
To a final full-stop. Look, madam; look, sir:
Bless all who are gathered together in this
Non-holy place. My hand is steady.

Some who are confused
shift and turn away thinking this trick unworthy
of folk who declined a life abroad:
a hand not for shaking, free of gifts, unmagical.
A trick, like the boxer early in the century, taut,
plucking a fly out of air.
But not this, not here. You turn away,
right, perhaps, to be insulted. Some buy time
(for the hand is steady) till it be urgent.
Who will tell us when it is urgent?

ii (a)

She wants to know his colour
the blind one, black or white:
what is he wearing today?

And we say to her:
think of things nearer your age,
think not seeing as your blessing.

She has outlived, out-thought us,
she will not play:
Priest's coat or surgeon's:
what is the butcher's colour today?

Because she is blind,
because she's now the daughter
of her daughter, punishing, punished

we listen. Through her
they have deprived us of sanity,
they have aborted our line

of argument. And we, near death
are patient, huddled
with those who wear our blood

white coats
black coats:
how can we embrace them like family?
How can we make them clean?

ii (b)

Here is another part of the wood.
On a morning before we were born,
or later in the day, the year,
the thing we strive to recall
broke the tranquility of this place.
None can remember when it ceased
being sacred. Some still worship here:
the barber cutting hair, the dentist
pulling teeth; others in from the sun.
(The musician and the dancer try to remind us
of what is lost – but they are outside).
The travelling merchant gains audience
of sorts. Some sit, a few kneel. And over there
bodies are being bared as if for healing.

And in he strides without guns or bombs,
without words that hurt, that kill:
how is it done, he's ridiculous –
a blind man approaching sex with a stranger,
alert both to charity and to ridicule:
he is not ridiculous

The musician and the dancer enter
to restore with memory time before pain.
We do not know how to dance to this music.

If we fail some will come
and hold a conference here
next year, each year
for years.

iii

We bring you news, of course,
From a far country. Bearers of gossip,
We have been moved on because
This late in the century, all
Have heard it. Safety in numbers, we come
With no more hope than a messenger bringing bad news
to Cleopatra. Some who have perished
Have been unlucky in their audience.

I bring you news
Not from obscure military men who force you
To mispronounce their names;
Not of mountains of skulls stored
By the last government, displayed by this one, used
To confirm theories, to discredit us all.
I bring no more news of slow, painful death
Of a people . . . we have had this
And have not used the knowledge.
So I bring you something manageable: this
From a far country not at war. Yes,
Fires have been lit in the house of your family.
Bullets in the backs of children have stimulated
Debate. For us, at the end of a century,
Who wish to influence debate, the price is high.
Let us sing.

iv

Even though it is this year, this century
and more of us are barren
and some who murder walk the streets
and are happy;
and friends grow shifty and turn away
from children (who have so long, so little
time to live);

and each of us can match a bad experience
told over dinner;
and glasses, dentures and other aids
now live with us

some resist
like a casualty of this group
draining away poison piped into the head,
or getting through the day without ache;
someone who might preach a sermon from this text
and think better of it.

Caribbean Woman Prayer

Wake up Lord
brush de sunflakes from yuh eye
back de sky a while Lord
an hear dis Mother-woman
on behalf of her pressure-down people

God de Mudder
God de Fadder
God de Sister
God de Brudder
God de Holy Fire

Ah don't need to tell yuh
how tings stan
cause right now you know
dat old lizard ah walk
lick land
an you know how de pickney belly laang
an you know how de fork ah hit stone
an tho it rain you know it really drought
an even now de man have start fuh count

de wata he make

God de Fadder
God de Mudder
God de Sister
God de Brudder
God de Holy Fire

Give me faith

O Lord
you know we is ah people
of a proud an generous heart
an how it shame us bad
dat we kyant welcome friend or stranger
when eat time come around

You know is not we nature
to behave like yard fowl

You know dat is de politics
an de times
an de tricks
dat has reduced we to dis

An talking bout politics Lord
I hope you give de politicians dem
de courage to do what they have to do
an to mek dem see dat tings must grow
from within
an not from without
even as you suffer us not
to walk in de rags of doubt

Mek dem see dat de people
must be at de root of de heart
dat dis place ain't Uncle Sam backyard
Lord, look how Rodney and Bishop get blast

God de Mudder
God de Fadder
God de Sister
God de Brudder
God de Holy Fire

To cut a laang story short
I want to see de children
wake up happy to de sunrise
an food in de pot

I want to see dem stretch limb
an watch dem sleep pon good stomach

I want to see de loss of hope
everywhere replace
wid de win of living

I want to see de man an woman
being in they being

Yes Lord
Halleliuh Lord!

All green tings an hibiscus praises Lord

Voice

I am the voice that often speaks
I am the words that often weep
I am the choice of sounds you hear
I am the echo heard every where.

We travel as one
And when you run
We're breathing in
And we're breathing out
To gain attention
We often shout.

Sometimes in your silent moods
You'll think of me
Before you decide
Before you choose

In the morning
When you sing and chant
Making the breakfast
When you know you can't.
I am the voice that never shouts
I am the voice you forget about.

I am the voice that often sings
I am the warmth beyond your lips
I am the rush of summer breeze
That lingers on like a floating leaf.

When you wake
YOU will yawn
I am the long tone
That tells you
It is dawn.
I am the voice that often speaks
I am the voice that often weep

I am the choice of sounds you hear
I am the echo heard every where.

Talk War

Talk War
War love
Love touch
Touch peace
Peace beat
Beat slip
Slip waste
Waste hate
Hate take
Take slice
Slice break
Break limbs
Limbs play
Play pain
Pain joy
Joy caress
Caress ploy
Ploy plan
Plan flight
Flight light
Light middle
Middle hand
Hand Wave
Wave ocean
Ocean land
Land walk
Walk destroy
Destroy War
War talk
Talk stop
Stop learn
Learn to
To breath

Breath love
Love touch
Touch peace
Peace.

'What have we got'

We got a mountain on the horizon
A sun on the floor
The sea in the sky
And the devil behind the door

We got a desert in a lake
An island in the city
We got the moon which is a fake
And a bomb which is a pity

We got stars when it is light
We got silence when it's not
We got friends but they fight
And what have we got?

We got brother in the sky
Sister in the sun
Everybody's getting high
No one is having fun

We got the rain-fall
We got the snow
Each brother we call
What do we know

'So Near and yet so Near'

There's a man who lives in a London apartment
And he's really blowing his mind
Says it's the fault of the government
And he thinks he's going blind
Because all he sees is darkness
But he says it's all a lark yes

There's a begger who lives on his weak so weak knees
And he says he's losing his head
Claims it's the fault of the zombies
And the people in power are the living dead
Says he thinks he's going to die
But he knows it's the living dead who lie

There's a teacher who lives in a school
And he says he's going wild
He says he knows what they are doing
And everybody is filed
He says he's going to learn
What the children should know
Says he's started to burn
But he cannot melt the snow

There's a policeman who lives in a cell
Says his jobs like living in hell
Says he must be heaven sent
'Cause he's the only one who knows it's bent
Yes he wishes he could fly
So he could leave and live in the sky

There's the old man who sits on the shelf
Says he's losing his wealth
And he could really care about his health
And he couldn't really care about his health
Just wealth . . .

There's the young boy who sits on the fence
Say sitting on the fence don't make no sense
Says he's going to have a child by a wife
Cut the fraction with a knife
There's always enough but no one will explore
The shadow behind the door
So near and yet so far . . .

Today Will Pass

Dew drops in the morning
The fallen tears of the night
Evaporate in the ever dawning
Streams of daylight

Here comes the day after
The sun climbs above the horizon
Cries turn to relief and laughter
A mirror reflects all around

When tomorrow leaves you
Then you will cry
But tomorrow stays by you
And today passes by

Look the other way to your fear
Happiness don't need an excuse
Flick away a fallen tear
Let go, get off and let loose

When tomorrow leaves you
Then you will cry
But tomorrow will stay by you
And today pass by

De Tongue (De First Instrument)

De tongue
was de very first instrument
When it was played
it caused a lot of excitement
Now it can be played good or bad
de sounds can be bubbly
or be sad
It has been known
to tell de truth
den agen de tongue
can lie like a brute

If yuh lie wid yuh tongue
it will get yuh inna muddle
and you will get trouble
pon de double
Nuh bother trouble, trouble
weh nuh trouble yuh

I play I tongue
to project de truth
and hope I can
inspire de youths
I wish I could play
Drums, bass and flute
den I could be a one man group
But it sticks wid I
night and day
most of de time yuh can hear it play

BUM BUH BUM CHA, BUH BUH BUM BUM BAH CHA
BUM BUH BUM CHA, BUH BUH BUM BUM BAH CHA
BUM CHA BUM BUM BAH CHA
BUM CHA BUM BUM BAH CHA

It can be polite
and it can be rude
But what is unique
about dis instrument
is it can also taste FOOD

■ QUOTE FEMINIST UNQUOTE POETRY

It is 1988 and I no longer feel I know what 'feminist' means. It is a word which, like 'hippy', has been part of common parlance in this country for the past twenty years – though, of course, 'feminist' has a longer, if intermittent, history. It is a word whose status has changed with the rapidly changing values of these twenty years. In some circles it has always been a dirty word: it is now one which I use with circumspection in circles – broadly speaking, left-wing or avant-garde circles – where I once used it, of myself, with confidence.

When it comes to 'feminist poetry', I suspect that, in the minds of most publishers' editors, the phrase is still synonymous with mere propaganda: only the marketing managers have realized that 'feminist' is a label that sells all kinds of books, including poetry.

In my own mind 'feminist poetry' is a phrase that has never sat comfortably. To put any sociologically descriptive tag – be it black, working-class, gay, lesbian or feminist – in front of poetry, is to limit its possibilities. To me, poetry must be one of the few areas of language use where it is acceptable, indeed obligatory, to try and break up the boxes we ordinarily think in and, in an increasingly computer-prone culture which values information and cognitive meaning above all, to reclaim the power of words to affect us emotionally and physically.

It was therefore with mixed feelings that I took on the task of compiling sixty or so pages of 'feminist poetry' for this anthology. From an initial list of fifty I chose the nineteen poets whose work is represented here by two or three poems apiece. I chose poets whose work I like and respect; I chose poems, some of which I have known and loved for a long time, some of which were new to me. In my own mind I let 'feminist' slide into 'woman', concentrating on the quality of the poetry, relying, for guidance, on my agreement with Adrienne Rich's resounding declaration that 'the daughter of the fathers is a literary hack'. My own definition of a successful feminist poem is one that is written by a woman with respect not only for her own 'truth', her own way of seeing and feeling the world, but also for the language – 'man-made' but not, given a little loving attention, unmalleable – which she uses to express that 'truth'.

I confronted my fear of the assumed need to be objective and representative in making choices. 'Objective' and 'representative' are, to me, man-made words or illusory concepts. Imagine an established body of published work commonly agreed to constitute 'feminist poetry and accompanying lit. crit. of the past twenty years': there would then be something to 'represent' here, something in relation to which my choice of poets and poems could be seen to be more or less 'objective'. But something like that is still in the making (and that's optimistic); something like this anthology has to contribute to its making.

In making my choices I employed a motley assortment of criteria or boxes-for-thinking-in, so that I would not end up with sixty pages of poems written by white English middle-class heterosexual women born since the war on the theme of nuclear power. There are no black women here – I 'gave away' the black and the 'experimental' poets I would have included to other sections in the book, because I wanted the anthology to have as many women poets in it as possible. The poets in this section represent, to my knowledge, six different 'countries of origin' and at least two social classes. Sexual orientation varies, and among the poets included are those who feel that their choice of lesbianism or heterosexuality is a significant component of self-definition and those who do not. Our 'themes' are multifarious: they encompass the recognizably feminist (abortion, sexism in husbands, the reshaping of Greek goddesses and the women of the Old Testament); the traditionally womanly (birth, childcare, the untrivially domestic); and the neutral ground of love, death, war, international politics, music, dolphins – and how *do* you classify *Crossing the Desert in a Pram*?

My conception of the feminist poetry of the past twenty years is ahistorical or non-chronological. In her poem *The Message* Jeni Couzyn writes: 'The message of the men is linear.' The message of the women has never in the history of Western literature been permitted to grow into and out of itself in a coherent way. The 'line' has been broken again and again. In the last twenty years the women's movement in America and Britain has led to the establishment of women's publishing houses which have made available feminist writings from the past that previously were not only unavailable but, often, had 'never been heard of'. It is now beginning to be possible to construct the 'line' in retrospect. Meanwhile, the feminist poetry of the last twenty years has been written – and published here and there, by mainstream and alternative publishers, in what still looks to be an extremely haphazard and piecemeal fashion. Chronology makes no sense, because there is no ongoing 'tradition', either long-term or short-term, to which the 'individual (feminist) talent' can be added. Moreover, there seems to be little correlation between a woman's age and the length of time she has been writing and the moment when she first achieves publication or 'intervention in the (established or alternative) literary tradition'.

Within the arbitrariness of alphabetical order I have tried to arrange the poems so that they lead into and out of one another. In doing this, I found very few places where there were sharp or jarring breaks in a kind of continuity that could perhaps be called 'collectivity'; something such as Eavan Boland describes at the close of *The Oral Tradition*: 'innuendoes, hints, / outlines underneath / the surface, a sense / suddenly of truth, / its resonance'.

I want the poets and poems included here to speak for themselves, in all their vivid variation.

Gillian Allnutt

Alien

'. . . *as a woman I have no country.*' Virginia Woolf

I have never returned
wounded, to the white cliffs
of Dover, knowing I rule –
though a bit of shrapnel
is my heart –
over and over singing
Elizabeth and England
in the bottom of
a gunboat.

No. I walk these streets
already beautifully paved
with bones of enemies
and women. I am subject
to a proud succession,
brave and noble sons
in mufti, bowler hats.

Who point to our great poets
with their walking sticks
of oak. Who will not bury
my heart in Westminster Abbey,
singing God the Father God
the Son and God the Holy Ghost,
this morning the serving maid
burned the toast.

Eliza sits below stairs to mend
the linen here in England's
green and pleasant –

and this land is my land
to which I have never returned.